THIS COLORING BOOK BELONGS TO

____

____

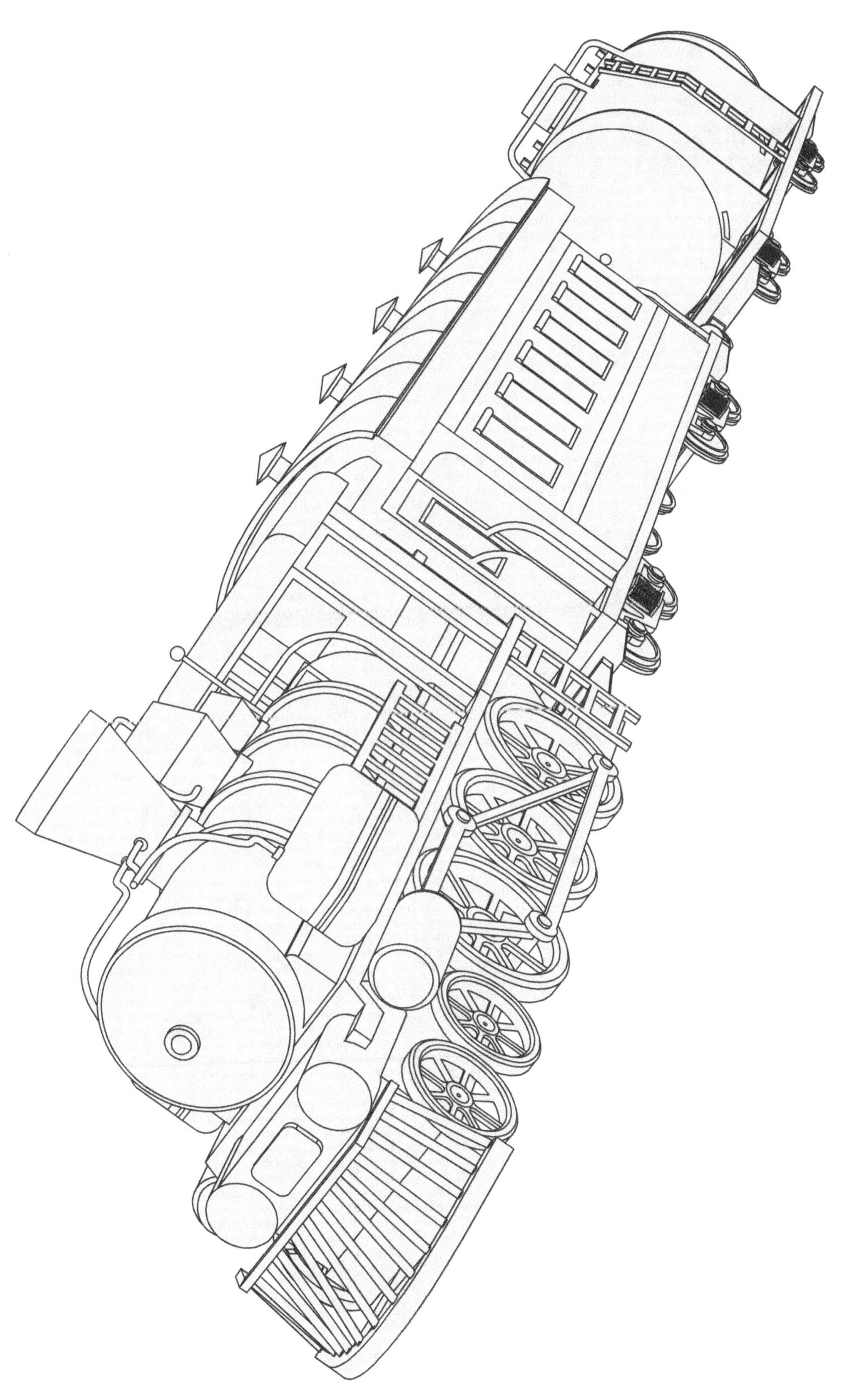

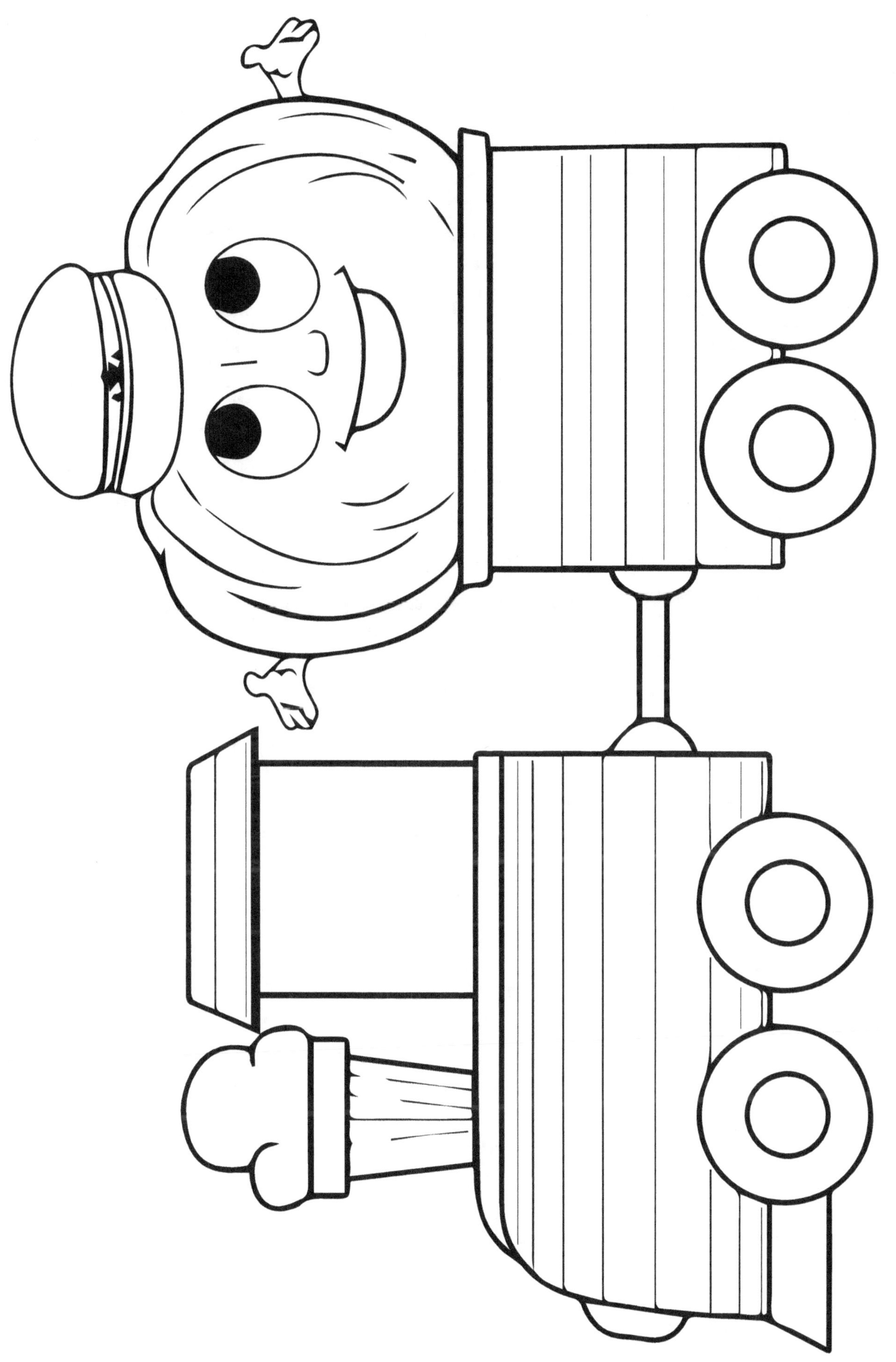

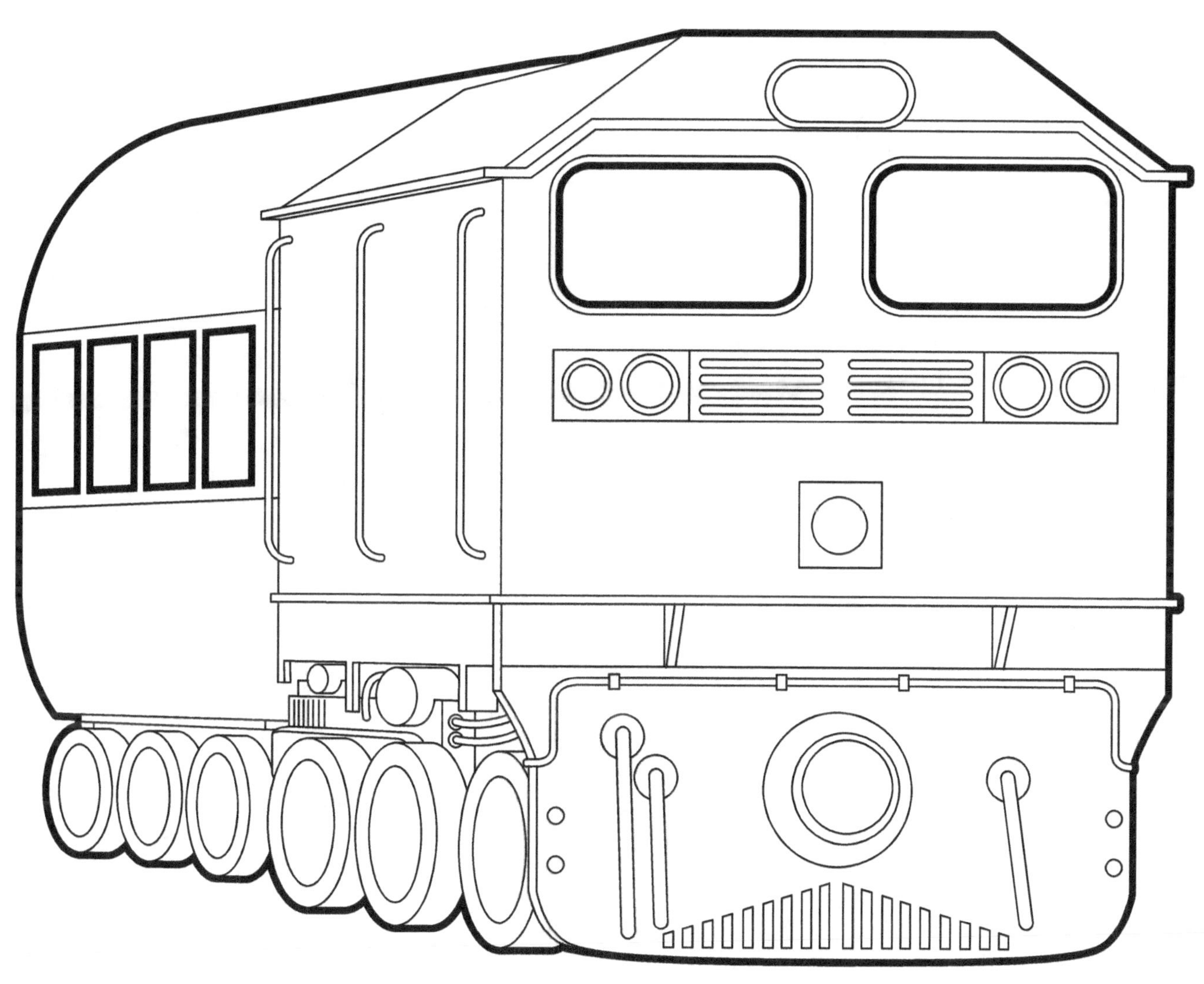

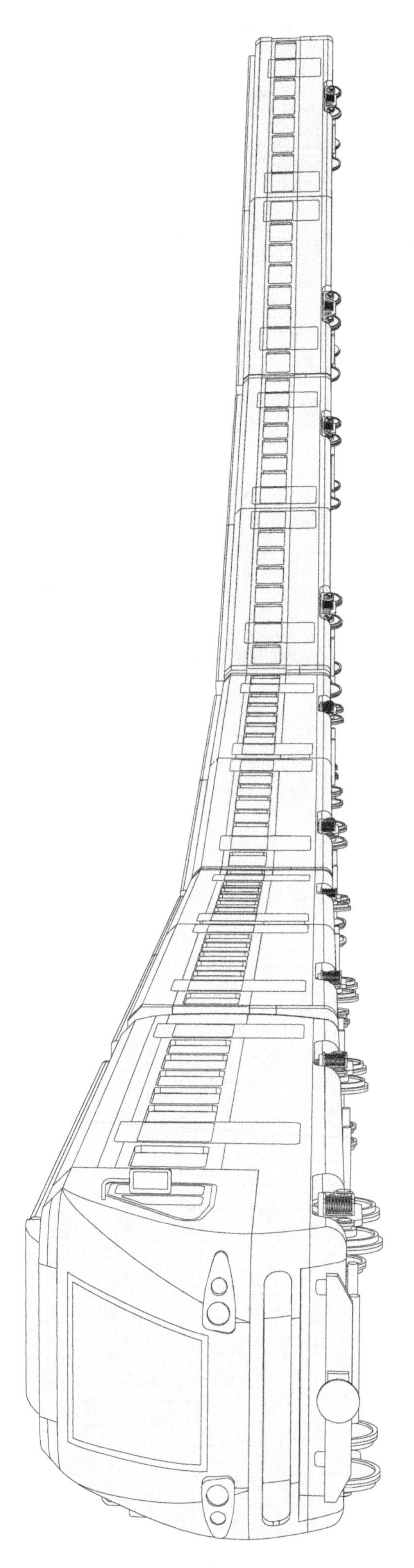

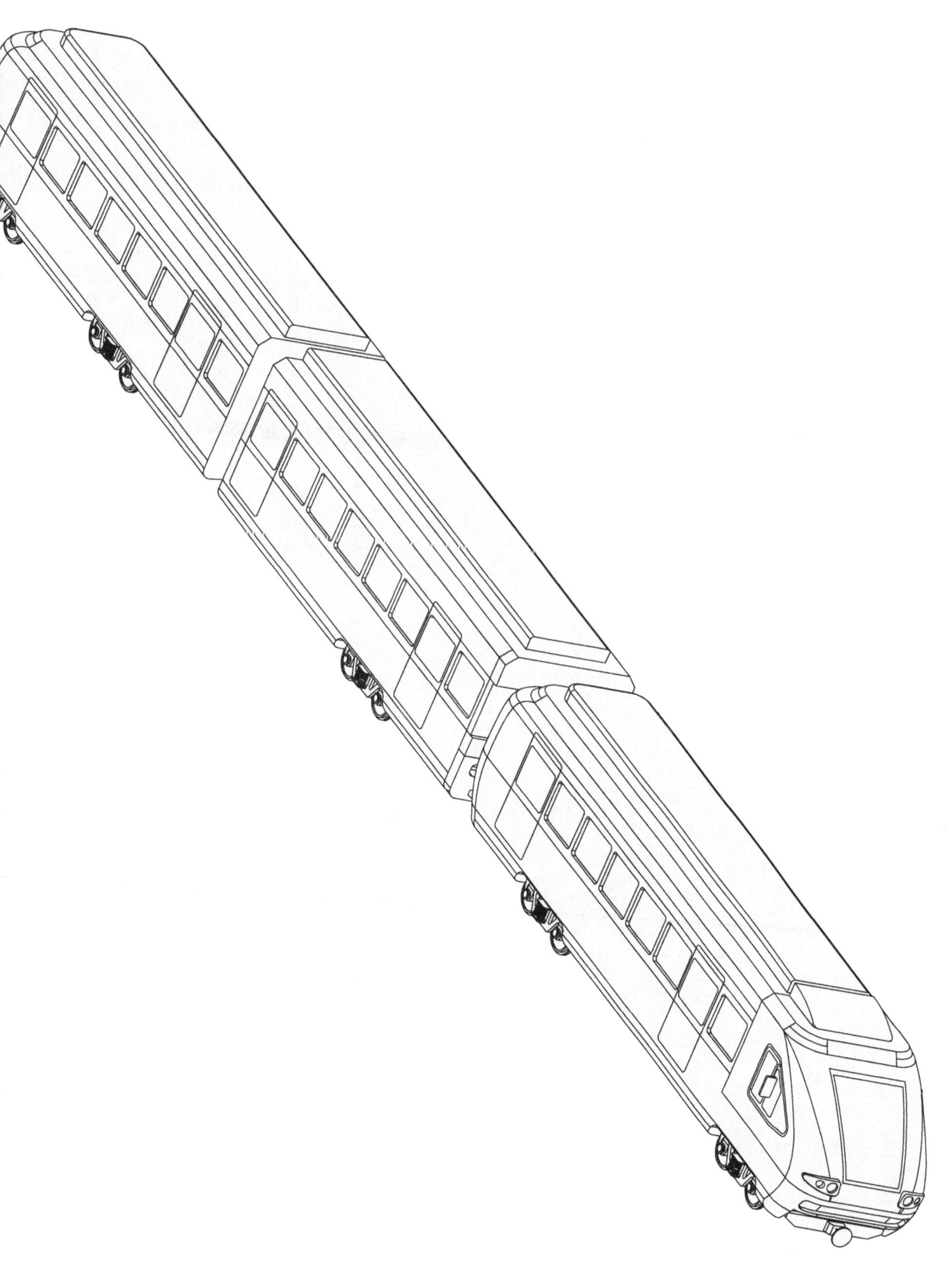

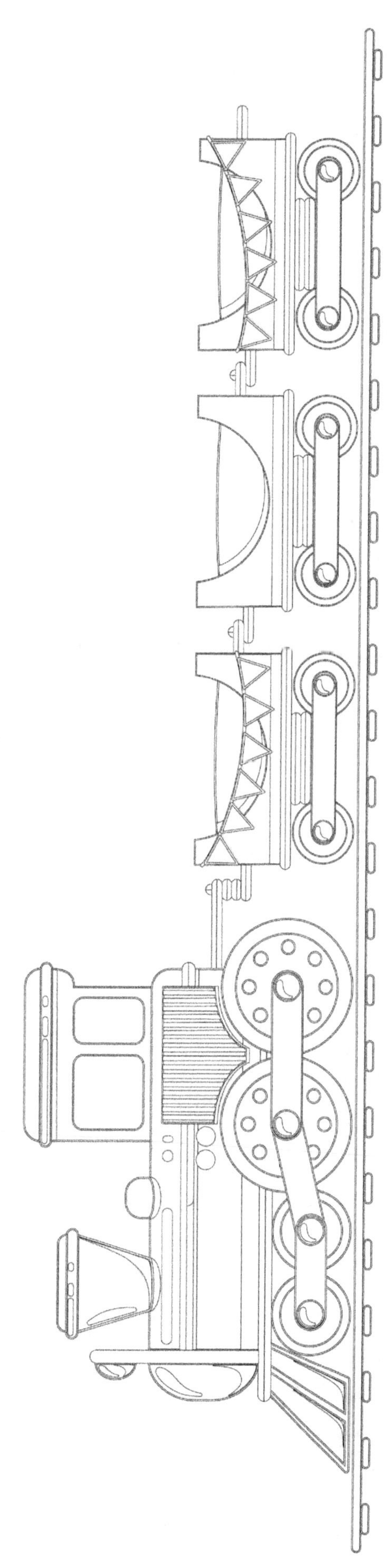

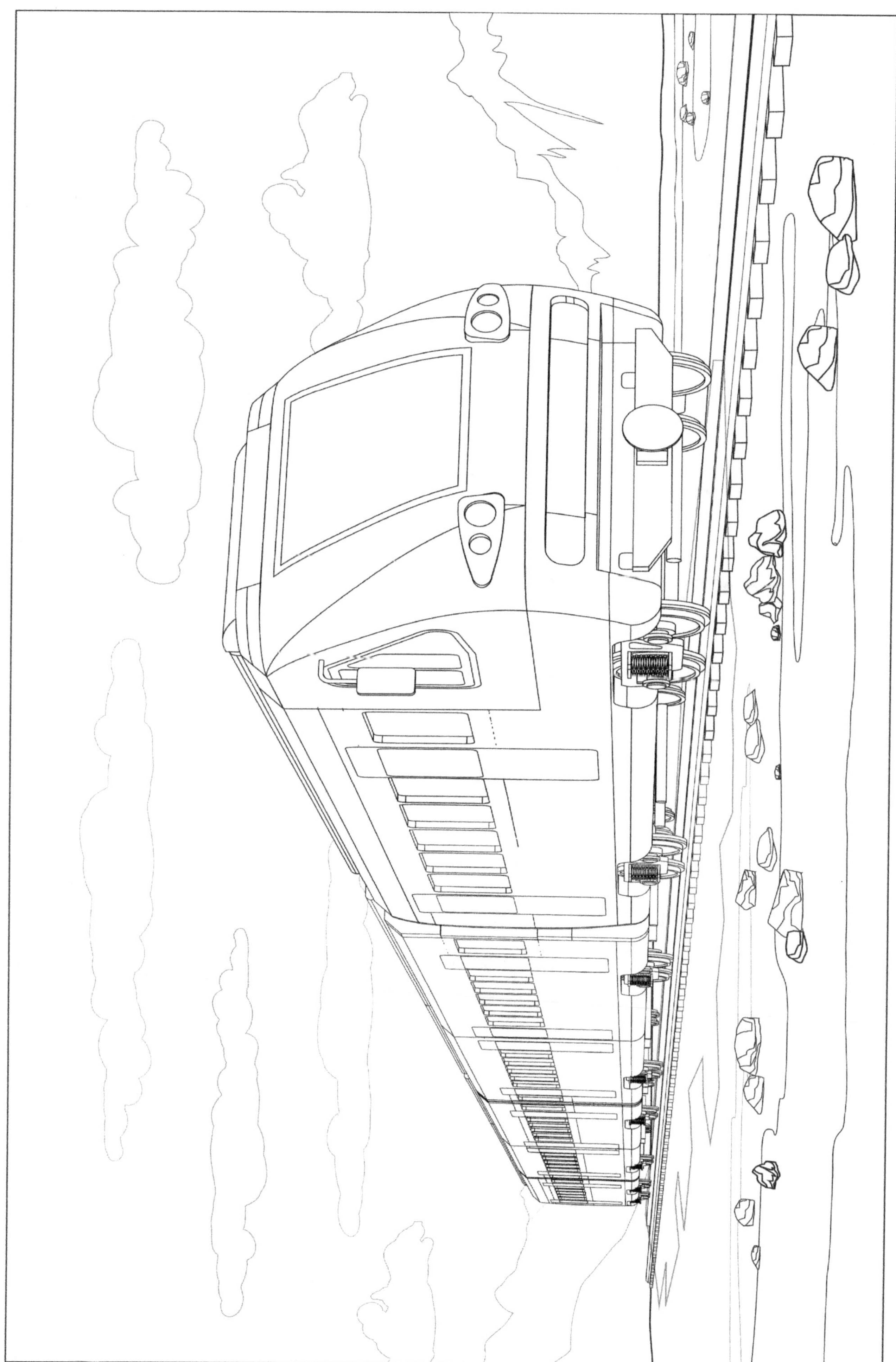

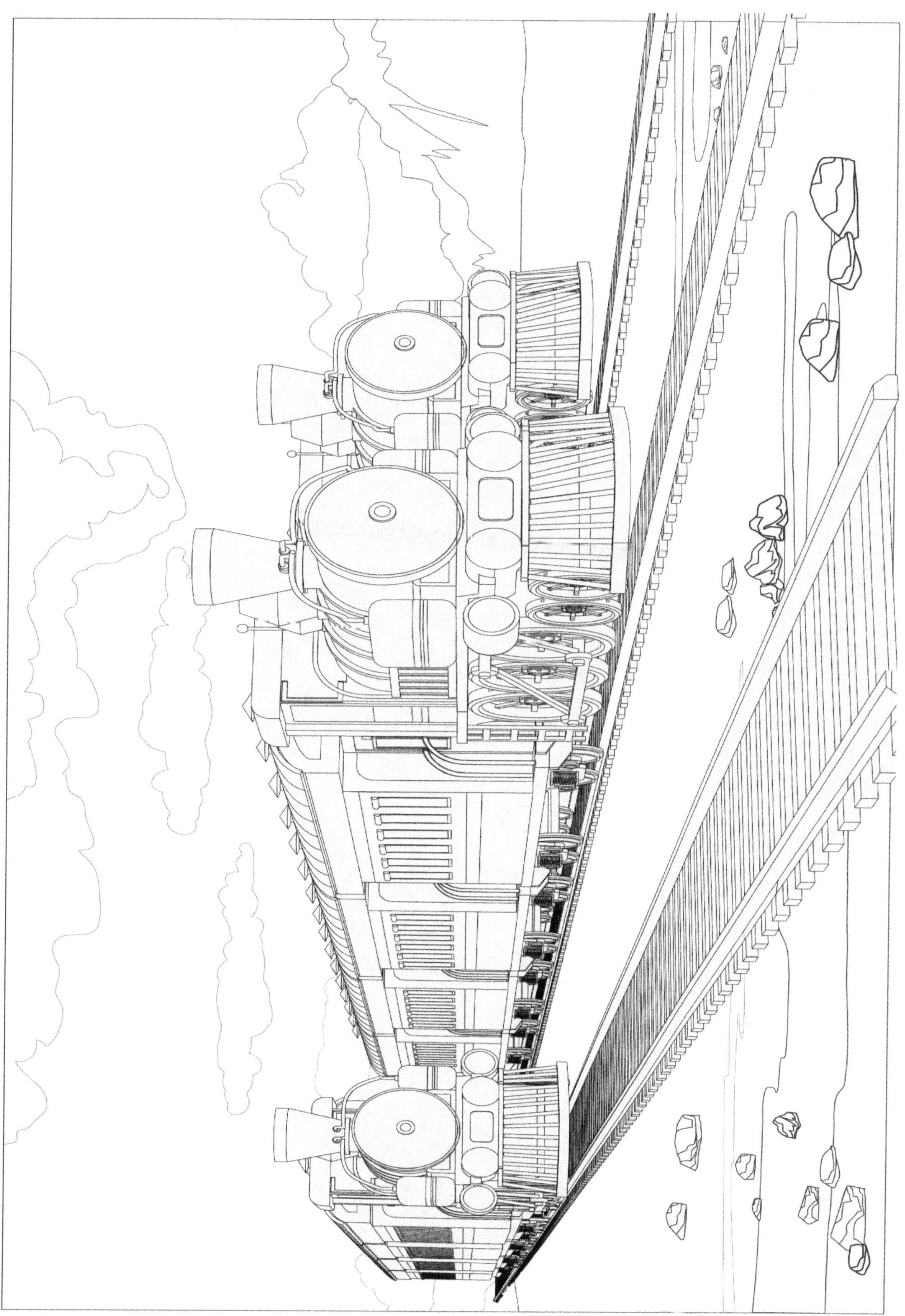

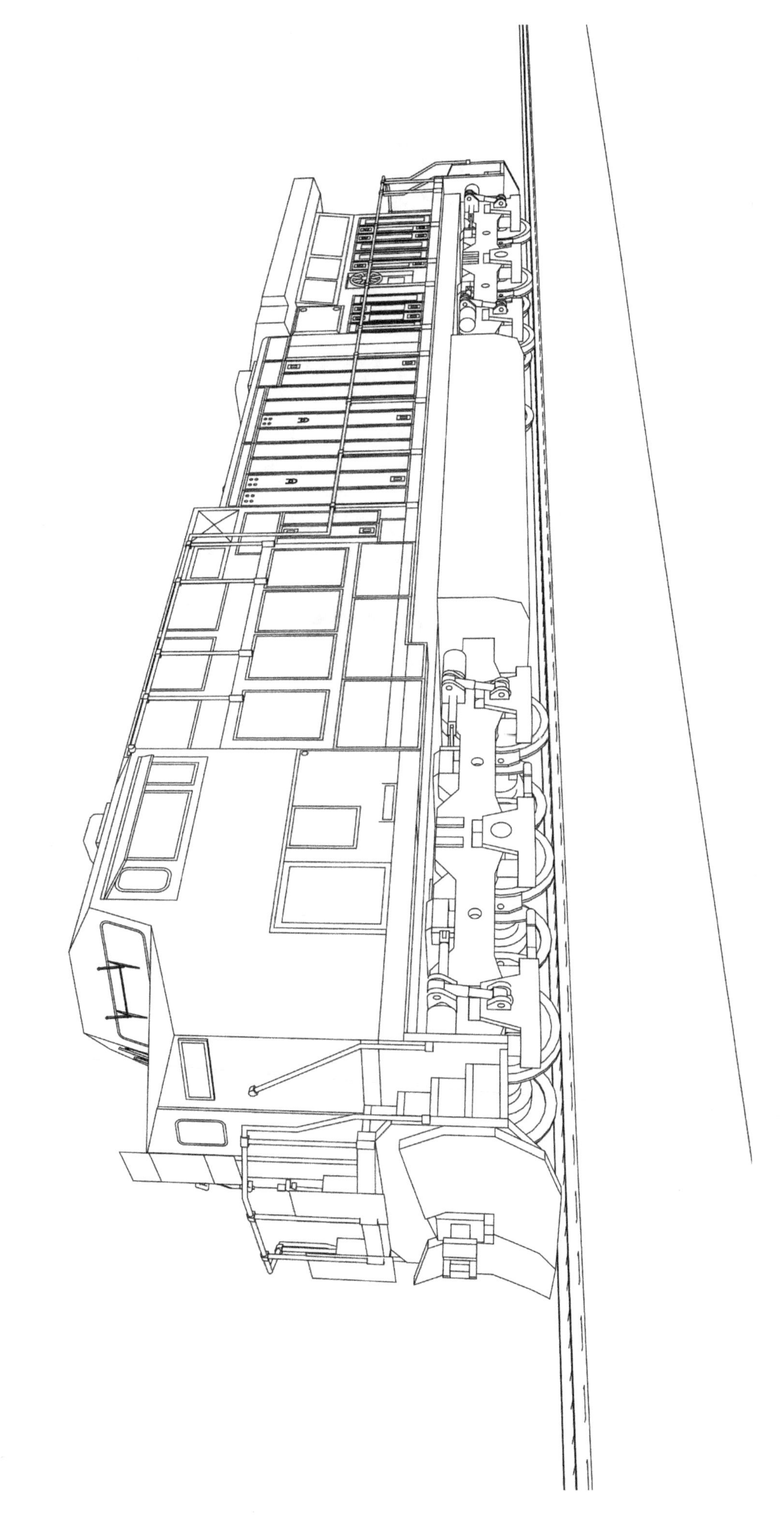